God Speaks in Many Tongues

MEDITATE
with
JOAN CHITTISTER
on
40 SACRED TEXTS

Benetvision

Erie, Pennsylvania

$6.00
Quantity discounts available.

355 East Ninth Street
Erie, PA 16503-1107

Phone: 814-459-5994   Fax: 814-459-8066
www.joanchittister.org
benetvision@benetvision.org

*Benetvision: Research and Resources
for Contemporary Spirituality* is a ministry of the
Benedictine Sisters of Erie.

Cover photograph: Stephanie Schmidt, OSB

ISBN: 978-1-890890-88-9

13 14 15 3 2 1

Introduction

I have been to dozens of international conferences but one I can't forget. At this gathering, organized by the Global Peace Initiative of Women we were all there—Christians, Jews, Muslims, Buddhists, Hindus and every variety of each. We came together as women, as professional religious figures, to bring women into the peacemaking arenas of the world in order to demonstrate the peace we sought in the religions we followed.

Clearly, then, this interfaith conference confronted us all with the challenge to make religion real. After all, we each and all—every single one of our traditions—preached peace. The question was, What were we really doing to bring it about?

Religion, we all had to admit, had done as much to breed wars as it ever had to bring the peace we said we were about. And where it wasn't the cause of the war, it did a lot to maintain it—as in Northern Ireland or Iraq or Israel or India. And multiple other places around the world.

But what would we do differently that could possibly not only break down the barriers between us but even create some real spiritual bonds? We were only women. Not politicians. Not preachers. Not negotiators. Not armed. We had not so much as a slingshot among us from which to disarm ourselves.

But then something happened that changed the entire conference, gave it truth, made it real.

The schedule called for a "Day of Prayer." Yawn. Who hasn't been to one of those? Nice but hardly earthshaking. Except that this one was different. In this day of prayer, every denomination, every major religious leader there, got up and led the conference in a prayer for peace from her own tradition.

At first, it seemed like it was going to be a long day of foreign recitations. Dull. But then, little by little, women began to join in. The singing got stronger; the chanting got fuller; the room got quieter, deeper, calmer. We weren't strangers anymore. We had honored a common God. We had honored one another's honoring. We had listened to another way of bringing peace, heard the message of it in another voice, lived in the same cosmic rhythm together and found it to be One.

God had taken all of us beyond our one tongue to the God of many tongues.

Our God had become bigger—and we, as well. The one God had brought us all into Oneness.

I understood something that day in a way I never had before: Beware the religion that turns you against another one. It's unlikely that it's really religion at all.

The effect of that day on my spiritual awakening is the impetus for this book, for this experience of meditative reading on the sacred texts of other traditions.

As I read each sacred text, I chose one phrase or a few lines that revealed a new understanding or raised a new question about God in my life. I recorded my reflection on each text and I invite you to do the same.

In using this book together may we listen to another way of praise, hear the message of God in another voice, and discover the sacred in all things.

May this little book help us break down religious barriers and create real spiritual bonds. May this little book be an adventure in finding new ways to see God and new ways to God.

–Joan Chittister

Meditation 1

Good people,
Most royal greening verdancy.
Rooted in the sun,
You shine with radiant light.
In this circle of earthly existence
You shine so finely,
It surpasses understanding.
God hugs you,
You are encircled by the arms
of the mystery of God.

Hildegard of Bingen

It may not be
official theological language
but it should be.

"God hugs you"
says it all:
When we're tired, depressed,
exhausted from working so hard,
full of satisfaction with today
but concerned about tomorrow,
God hugs you.

What else is there to say?

Choose a line from the prayer and write your own reflection.

_____

_____

_____

_____

Meditation 2

I am Peace
surrounded by Peace
secure in Peace.
Peace protects me
Peace supports me
Peace is in me
Peace is mine—
All is well.

Peace to all beings
Peace among all beings
Peace from all beings
I am steeped in Peace
Absorbed in Peace
In the streets, at our work,
having peaceful thoughts,
Peaceful words, peaceful acts.

A Buddhist Meditation

I must ask myself this:
Until I am peace,
what peace
can I bring to anyone else?

I must tell myself this:
Peace is the ability
to hear the other,
to reach out to the other,
to become the other.

Peace is about becoming
more than myself alone.

Choose a line from the prayer and write your own reflection.

_____

_____

_____

_____

Meditation 3

What actions are
Most excellent?

To gladden the heart
of a human being.
To feed the hungry.
To help the afflicted.
To lighten the sorrow
of the sorrowful.
To remove the wrongs
of the injured.
That person is the
most beloved of God
who does most good
to God's creatures.

The Prophet Muhammad

There is something very deceptive
about keeping rules.

Rule-keeping seduces me
into believing that I am holy—
when I am simply compliant.

It can make me
very judgmental of others.

Worse: It can make it impossible
for me to see my own limitations.

Rule-keeping may be the very thing
that traps me
in the worst of myself.

Choose a line from the prayer and write your own reflection.

_____

_____

_____

_____

Meditation 4

Who is fit to hold power
and worthy to act in God's place?

Those with a passion for the truth,
who are horrified by injustice,

who act with mercy to the poor
and take up the cause of the helpless,

who have let go of selfish concerns
and see the whole earth as sacred,

refusing to exploit her creatures
or to foul her waters and lands.

Their strength is in their compassion;
God's light shines through their hearts.

Their children's children will bless them,
and the work of their hands will endure.

Psalm 24 (version by Stephen Mitchell)

It is so easy to confuse power and authority.

Authority belongs to those
with the character, the wisdom
and the compassion to command it.
Power is only authority's cheap substitute,
claimed on the basis of ascendancy
and held only by virtue of force.

The world looks for authority
and is too often kidnapped,
hijacked or tricked by power.

Power lasts only as long as force lasts.
The authority that comes
with just being yourself
lasts forever.

Choose a line from the prayer and write your own reflection.

_____

_____

_____

_____

Meditation 5

*O Mother of the Universe, **glorious in all your forms and as the formless clear light of nondual awareness!** You alone are projecting various images of self and world for the evolution of consciousness, and you alone dissolve these images for the liberation of consciousness. You are mother and father, wife and husband, sister, brother, child, teacher, friend, and beloved. You are the single essence of all gods and goddesses, the single core of all religions. You are my True Self. You. You. Only You.*

Lex Hixon, Hindu

The face of God
is all around us
in everyone and everything.

There are no opposites, no other—
there is only
the presence of God in life,
in us,
in all.

So then why
do we insist on the divisions
that reduce the full face of God
to only our own?

Sad.
That is such a small God indeed.

Choose a line from the prayer and write your own reflection.

_____

_____

_____

_____

Meditation 6

How wonderful, O God,
are the works of your hands!
The heavens declare Your glory,
the arch of the sky displays Your handiwork.
In Your love You have given us the power
to behold the beauty of Your world
robed in all its splendor.
The sun and the stars, the valleys and the hills,
the rivers and the lakes all disclose Your presence.
The roaring breakers of the sea tell
of Your awesome might,
the beasts of the field and the birds of the air
bespeak Your wondrous will.
In Your goodness You have made us able to hear
the music of the world.
The voices of the loved ones
reveal to us that You are in our midst.
A divine voice sings through all creation.

Traditional Jewish Prayer

There is an ache
that comes in living.
It is the ache of Beauty seen
all around us
but, we know, even then
only half seen.

The beauty of God is both
the presence
and the promise.

I know the presence.

I am waiting
for the promise of it
now.

Soon, I'm sure. Soon.

Choose a line from the prayer and write your own reflection.

_____

_____

_____

_____

Meditation 7

Let nothing disturb you.
Let nothing frighten you.

All things are changing.
God alone is changeless.
Patience attains the goal.

One who has God
lacks nothing.

God alone fills all our needs.

St. Teresa of Avila

The presence of God within me
is the only stable center
of my life.

With it
there is nothing
that can destroy me or
leave me bereft,
confound or defeat me.

It is only a matter
of reaching out.

Correction:
There is nothing to reach for at all.
God is already here.

Celebrate.

Choose a line from the prayer and write your own reflection.

_____

_____

_____

_____

Meditation 8

Earth teach me stillness
as the grasses are stilled with light.
> *Earth teach me suffering*
> *as old stones suffer with memory.*
Earth teach me humility
as blossoms are humble with beginning.
> *Earth teach me caring*
> *as the mother who secures her young.*
Earth teach me courage
as the tree which stands all alone.
> *Earth teach me limitation*
> *as the ant which crawls on the ground.*
Earth teach me freedom
as the eagle which soars in the sky.
> *Earth teach me resignation*
> *as the leaves which die in the fall.*
Earth teach me regeneration
as the seed which rises in the spring.
> *Earth teach me to forget myself*
> *as melted snow forgets its life.*
Earth teach me to remember kindness
as dry fields weep with rain.

Ute Prayer

The courage
to be alone in life
is one of God's greatest blessings.

Then no words
can harm us,
no pain can deter us,
no resistance can discourage us,
no loneliness can destroy us.

Then we learn to live
in the memories of love
and the hope of tomorrow.

And that is enough.

Choose a line from the prayer and write your own reflection.

_____

_____

_____

_____

Meditation 9

*I vow to offer joy to one person in the morning
and to help to relieve the grief
of one person in the afternoon.*

**I vow to live simply and sanely,
content with just a few possessions,**
and to keep my body healthy.

*I vow to let go of all worries and anxiety
in order to be light and free.*

Thich Nhat Hanh

One of the greatest learnings
of life—
too often learned too late to enjoy—
is that to have as little
as possible
is the key to the happy life.

Only then can we move
from one stage of life
to another
with confidence
and contentment,
with nothing to lose
and everything to gain.

Only then are we really free.

Choose a line from the prayer and write your own reflection.

_____

_____

_____

_____

Meditation 10

Come, come, whoever you are,
Wanderer, worshipper, lover of leaving—
it doesn't matter.
Ours is not a caravan of despair.
Come, even if you have broken your vows
a hundred times
Come, come again, come.

Rumi

When we make the spiritual life
"a caravan of despair,"
we betray the God of life.

Life is a growth process
that melts us and shapes us
and brings us to the white heat of living well.

It is a long, long process—full of stumblings
and errors and failings and sins.

All of which teach us something
about ourselves, about living,
about becoming all we are meant to be.

Nothing is inconsequential to sanctity.
There is nothing to despair.
It is all a matter of choosing
to choose differently,
if necessary, the next time.

Choose a line from the prayer and write your own reflection.

_____

_____

_____

_____

Meditation 11

You will find that charity
is a heavy burden to carry,
heavier than the kettle of soup
and the basket of bread.

> *But you must your gentleness*
> *and your smile keep.*

Giving soup and bread
isn't all that you can do.

> *The poor are your masters—*
> *terribly sensitive and exacting*
> *as you will see.*

But the more demanding they seem
the more unjust and bitter
the more you must give them your love.

> *It is only because of your love*
> *only your love*
> *that the poor will forgive you*
> *the bread you give them.*

St. Vincent de Paul (adapted)

It is one thing to give charity,
that is the easy
indifferent part of it.

It is another thing entirely
to give the sense
of humanity and dignity
and personhood
that must go with the serving of the soup.

If the person you care for
leaves your care
feeling more of a person
than before you came along,
you have succeeded.

Only then.

Choose a line from the prayer and write your own reflection.

_____

_____

_____

_____

Meditation 12

In

my

soul

there is a temple, a shrine,

a mosque, a church

where I kneel.

Prayer should bring us to an altar

where no walls or names exist.

In

my soul

there is a temple, a shrine, a mosque,

a church

that dissolve, that

dissolve in

God.

Rabia, Sufi

Religion is the toxin
that too often poisons the idea
of the God in whose name we speak.

When we use religion
to divide, to demean,
to assert our own superiority,
then we have made ourselves
our religion.

Then God is shamed
and, possibly, ignored.

Then no one with a right mind
could possibly believe what we believe.

Good for them.

Choose a line from the prayer and write your own reflection.

_____

_____

_____

_____

Meditation 13

I believe in the sun
though it is late in rising.

I believe in love
though it is absent.

I believe in God
though He is silent.

Anonymous Holocaust Survivor

Not everything that is,
is always apparent.

Not everything we claim to believe
is seen to be alive in us.

It was not God who was absent
in the Holocaust.

It was we in whom the light of truth,
the love beyond tribes,
the god-likeness of the universe
was lacking.

Where were we then?
Where are we now?

Choose a line from the prayer and write your own reflection.

_____

_____

_____

_____

Meditation 14

I should like a great lake of finest ale
for the King of kings.
I should like a table of the choicest food
for the family of heaven.
Let the ale be made from the fruits of faith
and the food be forgiving love.

I should welcome the poor to my feast,
for they are God's children.
I should welcome the sick to my feast,
for they are God's joy.
Let the poor sit with Jesus at the highest place,
and the sick dance with the angels.

God bless the poor,
God bless the sick,
and bless our human race.
God bless our food,
God bless our drink;
all homes, O God, embrace.

Brigid of Kildare

The poor and the sick
are those who demonstrate
the secret sicknesses in us all.

In helping them,
we merit help for ourselves
when we are finally ready
to admit our deep needs,
our great gaping wounds of soul,
our desire to be fed,
to be loved,
to be helped,
to be made whole.

We are all in this together,
simply waiting for the other
to carry us along.

Choose a line from the prayer and write your own reflection.

_____

_____

_____

_____

Meditation 15

Tuncas'ila, I ask you
to hear my voice,
my prayers are always
for the future inheritors,
as we struggle to maintain
peace and healing upon our
sacred Grandmother Earth
on their behalf.

Arvol Looking Horse,
keeper of the white buffalo calf pipe

It is not enough
to take care of the present.
We have been doing that
for the last hundred years
to the point that we are impoverishing
the next hundred years.

It is time to realize
that the decisions we make now
teeter between betrayal of the past
and destruction of the future.

They fall on the shoulders
of the next generation, not ours.

Guilty or not guilty,
that is the question.

Choose a line from the prayer and write your own reflection.

_____

_____

_____

_____

Meditation 16

May I be happy, well and peaceful.
May my parents, grandparents and ancestors
be happy, well and peaceful.
May my brothers and sisters,
my spouse and children, my grandchildren
and all future generations be happy,
well and peaceful.
May all my friends and all my enemies be happy.
May all human beings sharing the earth be happy.
May all forms of life, plants, animals, birds,
fish and insects be happy.
May all sentient beings in the universe be happy.
May we all be free from suffering and pain.
May we all be free from attachment of greed,
anger and ignorance.
May we all attain perfect peace and happiness
of Enlightenment
through Buddha's Wisdom and Compassion.

Loving Kindness Meditation
–Reverend T. Kenjitsu Nakagaki

There are no ropes
so tight around the heart as greed.

There are no fires
so heated in the brain as anger.

There are no weights
so heavy on the soul as ignorance.

Greed constrains us.
Anger turns us to ash.
Ignorance drowns us in arrogance.

Be giving.
Be calm.
Be open.
Be.

Choose a line from the prayer and write your own reflection.

_____

_____

_____

_____

Meditation 17

*My Lord God, I have no idea where I am going. I do not see the road ahead of me. I cannot know for certain where it will end. Nor do I really know myself, and the fact that I think I am following your will does not mean that I am actually doing so. But I believe that the desire to please you does in fact please you. And I hope I have that desire in all that I am doing. I hope that I will never do anything apart from that desire. **And I know that if I do this you will lead me by the right road, though I may know nothing about it.** Therefore I will trust you always though I may seem to be lost and in the shadow of death. I will not fear, for you are ever with me, and you will never leave me to face my perils alone.*

Thomas Merton

If I always need to know
where I am going,
I will never be willing
to find new ways
to God.

I will never be able to learn from others.

I will never come to love the God of Surprises.

I will live only half a life
because the one God waits to give me,
I have refused to accept.

May God, most of all,
deliver me from my safe and cautious
self.

Choose a line from the prayer and write your own reflection.

_____

_____

_____

_____

Meditation 18

Today, like every other day,
we wake up empty and frightened.
Don't open the door to the study
       and begin reading.
Take down a musical instrument.
Let the beauty we love be what we do.
There are hundreds of ways to kneel
       and kiss the ground.

Rumi

The problem with goodness
is that it can become so dull,
so functional, so scripted, so smothering
that we lose touch entirely
with all the other ways
God has of showing us
what life is really all about.

Play a little. Laugh more. Try new things.
Walk through strange places.

God is waiting for you to find divinity
where you have never thought it could be.

God is waiting for you
to become spiritual
as well as simply good.

Choose a line from the prayer and write your own reflection.

_____

_____

_____

_____

Meditation 19

Be not lax in celebrating.
Be not lazy in the festive service of God.
Be ablaze with enthusiasm.
Let us be an alive, burning offering
before the altar of God.

Hildegard of Bingen

The god-life, the spiritual life,
is not an "exercise."

It is the intoxication
that comes with attending to the presence
of God in life.

It is the response of the heart
to that awareness.

It is the joy that comes with that trust.

It is the celebration of the daily divine,
which in our determination to control life
rather than to be consumed by it, we miss.

Let go. Let life. Let God.

Choose a line from the prayer and write your own reflection.

_____

_____

_____

_____

Meditation 20

Please, bless us,
who will gather around You, feeling so safe,
like baby birds that huddle
   under the wings of their mother;
wings that feel so incomparably soft
   from underneath,
although that mother-bird looks fierce
   from the outside,
with sharp beak and watchful eyes,
ready to protect its little ones.

Inspired by *108 names of Nrisimhadeva*
Devaki Katja Nagel

The need to be strong,
to be right, to be in control,
to be seen as powerful
can be the very thing
that stops us from looking into the self,
defining our own limitations,
and seeking the help we really need
to become the best of ourselves.

To come to the realization
that we are all simply weanlings
under the wing of God
frees us to grow and grow and grow
beyond our own paltry image of ourselves.

Then there is no room for regret
at the end.

Choose a line from the prayer and write your own reflection.

_____

_____

_____

_____

Meditation 21

Love is patient, love is kind.

It does not envy, it does not boast, it is not proud.

It does not dishonor others, it is not self-seeking,

it is not easily angered, it keeps no record of wrongs.

Love does not delight in evil

but rejoices with the truth.

It always protects, always trusts,

always hopes, always perseveres.

1 Corinthians 13:4-7

Love lies more in what I do
than it does
in what I do not do.

It is about what I do for others,
not simply about how I manage
my own inner thoughts.

Love protects the other
trusts the other,
hopes in the other
and perseveres in kindness.

Ah, love....

Choose a line from the prayer and write your own reflection.

_____

_____

_____

_____

Meditation 22

I bow to the Mother
Hail to the Golden Mother
Hail to the Black Mother
Victory to Ma Durga, the Mother of the World

Surround me with your loving arms...
> *hold me in your heart.*
Let me know that I am loved and that I can love.
Show me that no matter where I go
That I come and go in You.
I am never out of your loving presence.
That you are the smile behind the smile,
> *the touch behind the touch*
> *the kiss behind the kiss...*
You are the constant presence that I forget
> *until I remember*
and when I remember my Self, I remember You.
I sing your Name. What else can I think of?
You ARE Love.
And I AM You.

Translation by Krishna Das

There is no spiritual tradition in the world
that does not honor the feminine principle,
the female presence, in the cosmos.
    It is, it seems, the rumble of truth
    running in human veins everywhere.
How is it, then,
that the feminine principle
is derided,
the female is made invisible?
    On earth, only the male prevails,
    whatever must be said about the heavens.
Maybe that is why
there is so much violence on earth.
    Maybe that is exactly what is missing here.
Maybe nothing will change here
until we right the picture.
    Serves us right.

Choose a line from the prayer and write your own reflection.

_____

_____

_____

_____

Meditation 23

Teach your children
what we have taught our children—
that the earth is our mother.
Whatever befalls the earth
befalls the sons and daughters of earth.
If men spit upon the ground,
they spit upon themselves.

This we know.
The earth does not belong to us;
we belong to the earth.
This we know.
All things are connected
like the blood which unites one family.
All things are connected.

Whatever befalls the earth
befalls the sons and daughters of the earth.
We did not weave the web of life;
We are merely a strand in it.
Whatever we do to the web,
we do to ourselves.

Chief Seattle

If we spit upon the earth,
we spit upon ourselves.
    if we violate the waters,
    we violate ourselves.
If we rape the mountains,
we rape ourselves,
    if we savage forests,
    we savage ourselves.
If we choke the air
we choke ourselves.
    We are under suicide watch right now.
Someone should take
the belt, the bedcover, the drugs, the glass,
from our hands before it is too late.
    Madness that looks sane
    at one moment, sick at another
    is such a predictable disease.

Choose a line from the prayer and write your own reflection.

_____

_____

_____

_____

Meditation 24

Keep us, O God,
from all pettiness.
Let us be large in thought,
in word, in deed.
Let us be done
with fault-finding
and leave off all self-seeking.
May we put away all pretense
and meet each other face-to-face,
without self-pity
and without prejudice.

Grant that we may realize that
it is the little things of life that
create differences, that in the
big things of life we are as one.

And, O God,
let us not forget to be kind.

Mary Stewart

Smallness increases in proportion
to the greatness it derides.

Only the seriously small of mind,
the cramped of soul, the dull of heart,
demean another.

Only those who have little to parade
before the world,
set out to block the parade of the other.

It is the pitiable way
of those who cannot achieve in their own right,
who seek to build themselves up
by tearing the other down.

Smallness increases in proportion
to the greatness it seeks to belittle.

Maybe someone should tell them
it doesn't work.
Kindly, please.

Choose a line from the prayer and write your own reflection.

_____

_____

_____

_____

Meditation 25

O God,
Give me light in my heart
and light in my tongue
and light in my hearing
and light in my sight
and light in my feeling
and light in my body
and light before me
and light behind me.

Give me, I pray Thee,
light on my right hand
and light on my left hand
and light above me
and light behind me.

O Lord,
increase light within me
and give me light
and illuminate me.

Ascribed to Muhammad

We are born to find the light.
We live looking for light.

The problem lies in the nature of light:

We must remember that light is seeable
only in the center of darkness.

It is really guidance through darkness
that we pray for,
it is darkness that teaches the value of light.

It is darkness that tests the mettle
of the light in the soul.

It is darkness that makes us bold and brave
and tests our trueness
and makes us who we finally become.

Let there be Light.

Choose a line from the prayer and write your own reflection.

_____

_____

_____

_____

Meditation 26

*Lord, may we love all Your creation,
including all the earth and every grain of
sand in it. May we love every leaf, every ray
of Your light.*

*May we love the animals: You have
given them the rudiments of thought and
joy untroubled. Let us not trouble it; let us
not harass them, let us not deprive them
of their happiness, let us not work against
Your intent.*

*For we acknowledge unto You that all
is like an ocean, all is flowing and blending,
and that **to withhold any measure of love
from anything in Your universe is to
withhold the same measure from You.***

Adapted from a passage by Fyodor Dostoyevsky

❖

The sin of humankind
is the sin against its animals.
It is the sin of awful arrogance,
the sin of narcissism, the sin of pride.
It is the sin of those
who think that simply because we can love
that our love is without fault.
It is the sin of those
who think that simply because
our thoughts are higher
than the thoughts of animals
that our thoughts are pure.
It is the sin of those who believe that language
is the key to human superiority
despite the fact that we use language so well
to kill the heart of another,
to tell lies that destroy the other,
to plot evil against the good.
All of them, all of them sins against God.
What is so elevated about that?

Choose a line from the prayer and write your own reflection.

_____

_____

_____

_____

Meditation 27

May I be a guard for those who need protection
A guide for those on the path
A boat, a raft, a bridge
*   for those who wish to cross the flood*
May I be a lamp in the darkness
A resting place for the weary
A healing medicine for all who are sick
A vase of plenty, a tree of miracles
And for the boundless multitudes of living beings
May I bring sustenance and awakening
Enduring like the earth and the sky
Until all beings are free from sorrow
And all are awakened.

Dalai Lama

To awaken another to life
is to give the ultimate gift.

To awaken the other to laughter
is to give them freedom from fear.

To awaken the world to human community
is to make the world one.

To awaken the other
to the glorious complexity of life
is to enable them to grow up.

To awaken the other to hope
is to make every tomorrow a gift.

What better gifts than these
with which to face
tomorrow.

Choose a line from the prayer and write your own reflection.

_____

_____

_____

_____

Meditation 28

People are unreasonable, illogical,
and self-centered;
    forgive them anyway.
If you are kind, people may accuse you
of selfishness, of ulterior motives;
    be kind anyway.
If you are successful, you will win some
false friends; and some true enemies;
    be successful anyway.
What you spend years building,
someone will destroy overnight;
    build anyway.
If you find serenity and happiness,
others may be jealous;
    be happy anyway.
The good you do today,
people will often forget tomorrow;
    do good anyway.
Give the world the best you have,
and it may never be enough;
    give the world your best anyway.
In the final analysis, it is between you and God.
It was never between you and them anyway.

Prayer found on the wall of Teresa of Calcutta's room

Perhaps there is no pain quite so keen
as the suffering of seeing
what you spent years developing
ignored, forgotten, dismantled overnight.

It is right to cry.
After all, a life's work—
a living icon of the soul, a gift to the universe—
has been disregarded as lightly as a leaf.

It is not right, however,
to remain rooted in the rubble of it.

When the tears have finally dried,
begin again.
Once a message has been given
it cannot be ignored
no matter how deep the grave they dig
to conceal it from the ages.

Choose a line from the prayer and write your own reflection.

_____

_____

_____

_____

Meditation 29

Soham Soham Soham Soham
Om Om Om Om Om Om Om Om Om Om

I am neither mind nor body, immortal Self I am
I am witness of three states,
I am knowledge absolute
I am fragrance in jasmine, beauty in flowers
I am coolness in the ice, flavour in the coffee
I am greenness in the leaf, hue in the rainbow
I am taste bud in the tongue, essence in the orange.

I am mind of all minds, Prana of all Pranas
I am Soul of all souls, Self of all selves
I am Atman in all beings, apple of all eyes
I am Sun of all suns, Light of all lights.

I am that I am, I am that I am,
I am that I am, I am that I am.

Song of Vibhuti Yoga Sri Swami Sivananda

However smart we are,
we are not creators of ourselves.

We are children of the universe,
dust of the stars,
depth of the night,
slivers of the sun.

We come from the good of the cosmos,
from the breath of God.

We come from the Life
of Life.

Our task is one:
to pass life on, to live it well,
to reflect the maker in the clay.

Choose a line from the prayer and write your own reflection.

_____

_____

_____

_____

Meditation 30

Wherever I go, only Thou!
Wherever I stand, only Thou!
Just Thou, again Thou!
Always Thou!
Thou, Thou, Thou!
When things are good, Thou!
When things are bad, Thou!
Thou, Thou, Thou!

Hasidic song

Having come from God we are of the essence of God.

Nevertheless, unsatisfied. Restless,
seeking gain where gain does not lie,
we fail to see it.

Instead we strive to be like God
and are troubled when we fail
to grasp the ungraspable.

We ignore the essence of God in other people.

We allow the fullness of life
to slip through our toes like silt in water.

We grieve the death of the God
we have made for ourselves
and overlook the ground of God
that is already in us.

Choose a line from the prayer and write your own reflection.

_____

_____

_____

_____

Meditation 31

I am the one
> *whose praise echoes on high*
I adorn the earth
I am the breeze
> *that nurtures all things green*
I encourage blossoms to flourish
with ripening fruits.
I am led by the spirit
to feed the purest streams.
I am the rain coming from the dew
That causes the grasses to laugh
with the joy of life.
I am the yearning for good.

Hildegard of Bingen

It is at the point
of the yearning for good
that we touch
the spirit of God
within us.

When we have come to taste
a yearning for goodness,
when we become
the yearning for goodness,
we have become whole.

The rest of life
is simply a matter
of trailing good behind me
wherever I go.

Choose a line from the prayer and write your own reflection.

_____

_____

_____

_____

Meditation 32

I am of the nature to grow old.
There is no way to escape growing old.
I am of the nature to have ill-health.
There is no way to escape having ill-health.
I am of the nature to die.
There is no way to escape death.
All that is dear to me and everyone I love
are of the nature to change.
There is no way to escape
    being separated from them.
My actions are my only true belongings.
I cannot escape the consequences of my actions.
My actions are the ground on which I stand.

Buddha

We live in a world that teaches us to amass—
things, people, positions, titles—but for what use?

Who knows what clubs
     the Chinese student belonged to?
Who knows what house the woman lived in?
Who knows what money the crowd had to live on?

And who cares?

But everyone knows about
the standoff in Tiananmen Square,
And the sit-down in the Alabama bus,
And the free distribution of the loaves and fishes.

What will they know about us?

I don't know about you but I'm going to try
to leave some loaves and fishes behind.

Choose a line from the prayer and write your own reflection.

_____

_____

_____

_____

Meditation 33

To everything there is a season,
a time for every purpose under the sun.
A time to be born and a time to die;
a time to plant and a time to pluck up
that which is planted;
a time to kill and a time to heal;
a time to weep and a time to laugh;
a time to mourn and a time to dance;
a time to embrace
and a time to refrain from embracing;
a time to lose and a time to seek;
a time to rend and a time to sew;
a time to keep silent and a time to speak;
a time to love and a time to hate;
a time for war and a time for peace.

Ecclesiastes 3:1-8

It isn't that there isn't time to live
all the levels and dimensions of life.
It's just that most of us forget to try.

So we grow down instead of out,
rooted instead of flying.

Then we wonder
how life got painted in dreary colors
and how we grew to feel so dull inside.

But there's no use being alive
if you aren't alive.

Someone is waiting breathlessly
to check your pulse.
Do enough of something to develop one.

For all our sakes.

Choose a line from the prayer and write your own reflection.

_____

_____

_____

_____

Meditation 34

The world before me
is restored in beauty.

The world behind me
is restored in beauty.

The world below me
is restored in beauty.

The world above me
is restored in beauty.

All things around me
are restored in beauty.

It is finished in beauty.
  It is finished in beauty.
    It is finished in beauty.
      It is finished in beauty.
        It is finished in beauty.

Navajo Prayer

Regret is a holy thing—
if done well, if done little.

Regret tells us
that we know now that there were times
we could have done better.

And knowing that is best of all.

Then the past is really
"Restored in beauty."

It has been cleaned
and shined and purified.

It has done what the past is meant to do—
teach us, mold us,
lead us to an even better future.

Choose a line from the prayer and write your own reflection.

_____

_____

_____

_____

Meditation 35

Be at peace with your own soul,
then heaven and earth
will be at peace with you.
Enter eagerly into the treasure-house
that is within you,
you will see the things that are in heaven;
for there is but one single entry
to them both.
The ladder that leads to the Kingdom
is hidden within your soul....
Dive into yourself,
and in your soul you will discover
the stairs by which to ascend.

Saint Isaac of Nineveh

Who is it who doesn't know
exactly what their gifts are,
exactly what they lack in heart and mind and soul
if they are to be a fully developed adult,
a truly moral person, a person of spiritual worth.

In which case, there is no reason
to busy ourselves looking to others
for those answers.

The important thing is to admit myself to myself.

Then I can easily find
someone who can help me
find a way beyond the darkness
to the Light that is beckoning us
to the best of ourselves
even here, even now.
Always.

Choose a line from the prayer and write your own reflection.

_____

_____

_____

_____

Meditation 36

May the atmosphere we breathe
Breathe fearlessness into us:
Fearless on earth
And fearlessness in heaven!
May fearlessness surround us
Above and below!
May we be without fear of friend and foe!
May we be without fear
Of the known and the unknown!
May we be without fear
By night and by day!
Let all the world be my friend!

The Vedas, translated by Raimundo Panikkar

Oh, to be fearless, unafraid
of everything I have been taught
to fear:
the dark nights,
the white policemen,
the "colored people,"
the empty spaces,
the new faces,
the old enemies,
the strange places,
the great challenge,
the great failure,
the eventual losses,
the present possibilities.

To be unafraid is to live life
head back, arms out and running
toward the unknown.

Choose a line from the prayer and write your own reflection.

_____

_____

_____

_____

Meditation 37

O Lord,
open my eyes that I may see the needs of others,
open my ears that I may hear their cries,
open my heart so that they need not be
> *without comfort.*
Let me not be afraid to defend the weak
because of the anger of the rich.
Show me where love and hope and faith
> *are needed,*
> *and use me to bring them to these places.*
Open my eyes and ears that I may,
> *this coming day,*
> *be able to do some work of peace for Thee.*

Alan Paton

In an era when the choices are between
compassion and rugged individualism,
it is a moral imperative to choose
for the weak in the face of the strong.

Otherwise we will make a world
where one slight slip
on the economic ladder
will send a child into destitution
and a family into despair
and a country into oligarchy
and we ourselves into complicity
with those who measure people
by the amount of money they make
and the houses they buy
and the clothes they wear.

And then what kind of moral person
will we ourselves be?

Choose a line from the prayer and write your own reflection.

_____

_____

_____

_____

Meditation 38

Wearing a beautiful garland of forest flowers,
You shine like the light of the sun.
You are the Supreme Soul, the Supreme Light.
You are the Supreme Truth,
    and the Supreme Refuge.
Your Form is eternal,
    full of knowledge and full of bliss.

Inspired by *108 Names of Nrisimhadeva*
Devaki Katja Nagel

We hear so much about God
you would think that some people
found some primary data on the subject.

They sell their truth
with supreme confidence.

They tell small children
that God is watching them—
and keeping a record of the scenes.

They terrify everyone
and say that God tells them to do it.

But it is God who is Supreme Truth,
not those who claim to be.

Play it safe: Put your trust in God.

Choose a line from the prayer and write your own reflection.

_____

_____

_____

_____

Meditation 39

For as long as space endures
And for as long as living beings remain
*Until then **may I too abide***
To dispel the misery of the world.

The Way of the Bodhisattva
Shantideva

The great lesson of life
is this:

We were not brought here
for our own sake.
We were brought here
for the sake
of the rest of the world.

It is time now
to live
as if we know it.

Choose a line from the prayer and write your own reflection.

_____

_____

_____

_____

Meditation 40

Blessed are the poor in spirit,
for theirs is the kingdom of heaven.
    Blessed are they who mourn,
    for they shall be comforted.
Blessed are the meek,
for they shall inherit the earth.
    Blessed are they who hunger and thirst
    for righteousness,
    for they shall be satisfied.
Blessed are the merciful,
for they shall obtain mercy.
    Blessed are the pure of heart,
    for they shall see God.
Blessed are the peacemakers,
for they shall be called children of God.
    Blessed are they who are persecuted
    for the sake of righteousness,
    for theirs is the kingdom of heaven.

Gospel of St. Matthew 5:3-10

Those who make peace in a warring world
are more priceless than the price
of all the weapons we use to make war.
Those who make peace in the face of bigotry
are co-creators of a world
not yet aborning.

Those who make peace
in the face of discrimination,
and money, and hatred, and spite
are those who save the world from itself.

May they come soon—in numbers,
unarmed, open-hearted, and laughing.

Then let the world
dance a victory dance.

Only then.

Choose a line from the prayer and write your own reflection.

_____

_____

_____

_____